Freefall –
Pushing it to the
Edge

Freefall – Pushing it to the Edge

Donnie MacDougall

Print information available on the last page.

Rev. date: 11/04/2020

To order additional copies of this book, contact:
Xlibris
UK TFN: 0800 0148620 (Toll Free inside the UK)
UK Local: 02036 956328 (+44 20 3695 6328 from outside the UK)
www.Xlibrispublishing.co.uk
Orders@Xlibrispublishing.co.uk
742144

Contents

Acknowledgements

Thanks to my ex-wife Marion, my family and friends, Raymond Robson, Europe's top cranial osteopath John Page, hypnotherapist Paul McKenna, Dr Richard Bandler, the great work done by the air ambulance, Ward 20 at Dundee Royal Infirmary and Ward 5 of the Bridge of Earn Hospital.

I have faced doom and gloom, but I am bouncing back thanks to my DNA.

Introduction

This story is a way of acknowledging those who have helped me along the way. It might seem a bit patchy and it might jump around, but it is how my injured brain has remembered things. Fortunately, as I continue to receive treatment and make progress, my memory has started to improve.

Telling my story has allowed me to reflect on how far I've come since my accident and also the fact that I have been supported by the very best, to whom I can only say a truly heartfelt thank you.

Chapter One

My Family and Growing Up

My name is Donnie MacDougall and I was born in Gask, Scotland. My parents were Donald MacDougall and Rita MacDougall, and I have a younger brother, Gary, and an older sister, Sheila. My dad had two brothers (Dougie and Alistair) and a sister (Flora). Mum had a brother (named John) and a sister (Jean).

Dad's father was Willie, and his mum was Kaleena. I never met my mum's dad, but I do know that he was a successful businessman with Sutherland & Watt Chemical Spraying Company up in Blairgowrie. When Mum was little, her parents divorced and she was presented with a choice of either staying with her dad, or going south to Gask with her mum, brother and sister. Of course, she chose to go with her mother.

My mum was a great person. She worked as a cleaner in local schools and she also cleaned the houses of various people in the area. She was always ready to give assistance to anyone who needed it and, just like my dad, she enjoyed working. She had the work ethic, but I have to say the biggest influence in my life has been my dad.

When Sheila, Gary and I were just kids, as a family we moved into an old two-storey house in Clathy Gask. It was quite rundown and needed doing up, but my parents had some very good mates and together they did all the renovation work. In the end, they did

1

a great job and turned that dilapidated house into a fine family home.

The house had a garage with a pit for working on cars, which was useful because Dad loved sorting out car problems, especially when nobody else knew what was wrong with a vehicle. It became like a puzzle for him to solve. People would call at the house, leaving their car running outside, and then Dad would have a look at the car so that he could, in most cases, quite quickly tell the owner what needed fixing. He used to spend all his spare time out there repairing cars and, in doing so, he taught me all about working on engines.

Right from when I first learnt how to walk, I used to be in there with Dad, watching him at work. In fact, I was still very young when he taught me to drive cars and trucks and to operate the different machinery he had. I soon became so capable at driving that when Mum used to go out to play darts and dominoes with her friend Georgie, at the end of the night she'd say that it was probably safer for me to drive them home than for them to do it! It was good for building up my experience.

Dad worked for Dow Brothers, who used to have a big garage at the bottom of Victoria Road in Scone. His main job was as a driver, but he was also an electrical-mechanical engineer, which meant he could repair and service the trucks as well. He loved working on machinery and would do that all hours of the day and night. Dad used to take me to the garage.

When we were kids, my sister and I would spend much of our time with our dad's mum, Granny Kaleena, down in Blair Drummond. Granny's home was where all the grandkids could meet and we'd get to see our cousins there. Later, when I was about 12 or so, Granny moved to Gargunnock, out by Stirling.

My early years were pretty active, being mostly spent outside with my mates, building gang huts, making rafts and that sort of thing. We would be miles away from the house during the day and we would often camp out overnight. There was also a big airbase up in Mayfield and we'd go camping there too. In those days, life was like that for children, but parents don't let their kids do such things nowadays.

One friend's family had a farm and I spent some of my time there, working with the tractors and farm equipment. Another friend's father started his own trucking company and my dad even owned a truck at one stage. What with the farm, the trucking business and Dad's cars and job, you could say I was brought up with big machinery all around me. From our living room window, I could even see an old wartime runway and it completely fascinated me. Due to Dad's influence, I had opportunities to learn all about such machinery from a very young age.

As well as taking me to the garage – and again while I was still very young – Dad used to take me with him when he went out driving and we went all over Scotland and sometimes as far afield as Europe. The lorries he drove were pretty big because they were used for transporting plant machinery and, in later years, he started a job delivering meat. I used to love going away with him, especially as it was an opportunity to learn all about the plant machines and the trucks – all of which became important to me when I was older. Because of that experience, I had no doubts about what I wanted to do when I started going to work and I was confident that I could make very good money in the plant machinery and truck business.

We used to have family holidays in Morecambe, Portsmouth and other places all over Britain. Uncle Alec, who lived in Portsmouth, was an electrician and was in the navy, so we often visited him, Auntie Margaret and their two kids, Debbie and Kevin. I liked going there, especially because Uncle Alec was a very sociable person and he knew how to enjoy himself. On another holiday, Dad took my sister and me on a day trip to Cherbourg, France, which, with it being abroad, was pretty exciting for us kids.

By that time, Dad was travelling all over Europe, driving refrigerated trucks to take meat from Perth to European cities. I loved going with him, seeing life in Germany and France. Dad knew his way around all these countries.

All in all, I had a very good childhood growing up around Clathy Gask. I went to a very small primary school with only 30 or so pupils. It was so small that, because some of the boys were so wee and some of the girls wouldn't want to play, we didn't have enough people to make a team for games such as football or cricket. When the time came for me to move on to secondary school, I went to Auchterarder, which meant I suddenly had quite a journey. In the mornings, whatever the weather, we'd have to walk three miles down to the end of the brae to catch the bus to school and then, of course, it was the same thing again on the way home in the opposite direction, making it six miles in total every day. They were certainly different times, and you wouldn't see kids doing that today. Even to get to the primary school at

Findo Gask we had to walk exactly a mile there and back – quite a long way for little legs, but it was a great way of keeping us very fit and that helped me in later years.

Chapter Two

Teenage Years in Auchterarder

As soon as I turned 16, I left school, moved to Auchterarder, living in the best digs with Bill and Joan, and took a job as a painter-decorator. I had wanted to be an electrician, but the wages were only £13 a week, whereas a decorating company, Hally, was offering me £25 a week and any overtime was paid at double-time. Needless to say, I jumped at the opportunity. That £12 between the two weekly wages doesn't sound much today but it was a massive difference at the time. I was expected to work for it, though. Right from day one, the boss made it clear that I was there to learn, not simply to make the tea, and learn I did. Within a couple of years, I was a very competent painter. That company was very good to me. In the end, though, I only stuck at the painting and decorating with Hally for two years because I had what you might call a 'difference of opinion' with my boss.

As a young lad, I used to love going to watch the football, although I didn't play much myself, preferring to watch the experts and then socialise with my mates from Auchterarder afterwards. We often went into Glasgow with David and Robbie to watch Rangers and even when I was still at school, I liked the lifestyle there. We were pretty devoted followers, too, because we'd follow the team around the country, going as far as Aberdeen, Kilmarnock and Dundee. Sometimes we even went to Europe if it was a big match. It was a great way to meet up with my friends, including a good mate Steve. I will not say what we called him, but he knows (ha ha!). It was a very sociable time, especially as they would know all the right places and the best pubs to go to. I used to love going out in Glasgow and Edinburgh, and, even in the early 1980s, Perth was an excellent place for a night out. We'd go to all the discos to dance, meet girls, enjoy a drink or two and have fun. I enjoyed Auchterarder. I would meet up with good friends such as Steve, Donna, Angela, Alison, Fiona, Brian, Michael, Kevin etc.

Anyway, back to Hally. On this particular occasion, I was planning to go to Düsseldorf in Germany, to watch Rangers play, but I needed some time off work to do so. When I went to ask the boss, much to my surprise and annoyance, he said to me, "We need you here; we're too busy to let you go." I ended up jacking in the job there and then. After that, I was off to the football but, of course, when I returned home, it hit home that I no longer had a job.

Chapter Three

Moving to Perth and Learning to Skydive

When I was still only 17, I moved to Perth and began doing fencing and laboring jobs. What I really wanted was to work in the plant business, but I knew I would have to pass my driving test first because the bigger plant jobs are always on the outside of cities, on major roads, such as the Edinburgh bypass, which meant I would need to drive to the sites every day.

Before I could drive, I used to take the bus to St Andrews and I enjoyed my time with Marion and her good friends Debbie, Sandra, Linda and Irene. I would meet up with Pete, who was in the Royal Marines 45 Commando Condor, near Arbroath, and have some great nights with Pete, Paul and Ian.

I soon obtained my driving license and started with Morris Young, as I wanted to work on the plant machinery. I was with Morris Young for nearly four years. In 1984 or 1985, we were working on the Edinburgh city bypass, where I drove a Liebherr 942 digger and the machine that lifted the big shutters into place on the site.

One day, the ganger, Andy Gibson, said to me, "Donnie, I've been talking to Billy. [I knew Billy had won a few British and European skydiving awards.] Do you want to go next week? We're having a long weekend and, if you want, I can arrange for you to do your first jump."

I didn't need to be asked twice because skydiving was something I had always wanted to do, and not just for the social side. As I've said, I loved going to the football but didn't play much, preferring the socialising around it but with the skydiving, it was different. I had become fascinated by skydiving at that stage and I used to talk about it at work all the time. The jump was arranged and off I went. It was amazing and as soon as I had done it, that was me hooked for life.

In 1985, I did my first jump. I was just 22 years old.

The jump was originally scheduled for the Friday – the whole day had been spent doing the training, learning how to skydive. I was there at first light in the morning, dead on 7.59am and 25 seconds, and the adrenaline was pumping through my veins. It was a magical day. Forget cloud nine, I was on cloud 10 and ecstatic at the thought I would be jumping in a couple of hours' time. The anticipation was at fever pitch.

There were six of us new recruits, so we were kitted up and then we filed into the aircraft ready for take-off, senses buzzing. Up we went and, at 2,500 feet, when I looked out of the plane door, I immediately recognised the area where I had grown up, including my old school. From that height, it looked like a tiny model village. I couldn't dwell on it, though, as in the next few minutes, we were going to jump. I was steaming with excitement, sitting there with my boots dangling out over the edge of the aeroplane doorway. I had to pinch myself that it was real, that I was actually about to jump for the very first time in my life. It was completely thrilling and I knew there was no turning back as I gasped deep gulps of the cool air coming into the plane from outside. I had no choice; I closed my eyes and started counting. I was ready to fulfil my destiny.

Then suddenly a radio message began to crackle in the background. The mission was to be cancelled – with immediate effect.

I'm sure my jaw must have dropped all the way down to the ground, with no parachute deployed! I was gutted to the core. In that split second, my dream had died. The excitement was over.

I was furious as I hurried home that night and when I arrived, I just threw my keys on the breakfast bar. I was inconsolable. Then the phone rang. It was Johnny, from the airbase. I assumed he was calling to commiserate with me, but no. The jump was back on, tomorrow at dawn – I shrieked with joy!

I was first to arrive there the next morning and conditions were looking excellent for my first jump. The same crew assembled in the aircraft and we were soon back at altitude. All six of us were rookies and we sat in rotation procedure. We were full of anticipation, shifting about on the benches, unable to remain still. The first person went, then the next, the next and the next. I was the last to jump and as I sat opposite the door, I watched them fall, seeing below me the thrill on their faces. By this point, I was buzzing – I wasn't at all scared, because the adrenaline and the overwhelming feeling of excitement had taken over. The instructor tapped my shoulder. That was the signal that was to change my life for ever.

Throwing caution to the wind, and with a wing and a prayer, I pushed myself out. The thrill was instant. The wind whooshed around me as I fell through the air. I hurtled downwards at speed, arms outstretched, yet seemingly suspended in the moment. As you fall away, you're still attached to the plane by a static line. The canopy is pulled out of your harness, and then your parachute is pulled out of the canopy so that it trails behind you. As soon as the parachute is fully deployed, the static line breaks and ends your connection to the plane. You're then free. The canopy is open, and you are falling. You should be counting, "1,000 ... 2,000 ... 3,000 ...," before shouting, "Check canopy!" as the chute unfolds itself fully and silently in beautiful red and white. At 2,000 feet, you bring in your hand to pull the dummy handle.

I felt a great sense of accomplishment as I floated gently back to *terra firma*. It had gone perfectly, so perfectly that I wanted to do it all over again – and again and again. Unbelievably, the whole rookie team immediately demanded ecstatically to do it again and, lo and behold, before nightfall, we had all parachuted twice and on our first day too.

For the first few dives, the instructor stands at the door of the plane, watching to ensure you are doing everything correctly. He checks to make sure your body is in the correct arch, and he listens to what you are saying as you drop. If you pull the dummy handle correctly each time and make the right arches, then you can go on your first freefall skydive. After that, when you have completed three error-free freefall dives, you can then do the five-second delay dive and if you do that correctly, you move on to the 10-second delay. The feeling is incredible.

In 1989, I was dragged, without much protest, to France for a whole week of continuous skydiving. Luckily, the weather at Laferté was stunning so it was very busy; in fact, I had never seen so many people jumping out of various aeroplanes all day long. In the canteen people of all nationalities and abilities queued for the delicious food that was on offer. Everyone was upbeat and it felt like a real holiday. As the days passed, I progressed through the categories rapidly so that, by the end of the week, I only had a few more jumping tasks to complete to achieve Category 8, at which point, I would lose my novice status. I had learnt well and was keenly aware of the dos and don'ts which form the essential code of conduct for the skydiver.

Billy, who knew the French jumpers well, was asked if he would like to try out the latest, most advanced small canopy on the market, the Wildfire. He enthusiastically jumped at the offer. The French knew he was very capable, yet they cautioned him about the turning capabilities of this chute as his descent would be rapid. I watched mesmerised as Billy descended at a speed we hadn't seen with any parachute before. Jocky – my friend and one of the world's most adept and qualified skydivers with over 15,000 jumps – commented, "Wow, they are going to have to be careful as to who is allowed to use that chute. It is lightning fast!" Part of me wished I could be allowed the chance to do it myself, while another part of me thought there was no way I would do it, even in the future, because it was way above my capabilities.

All too soon, it was time to leave for home, although I was missing my wife, who was heavily pregnant, and my little lad. Despite feeling a little guilty, I was nevertheless determined to return to France for more skydiving as soon as I could. We flew out of Charles de Gaulle on a sunny Thursday, arriving back in Edinburgh and then home.

The year 1985 didn't only see my first jump, it was also the year I married my wife Marion. Marion is very family orientated and even when we first started going out together, she used to talk about having a boy and a girl, wondering what they would look like. In the following years we found out when we had a son, Mark, in February 1987 and a daughter, Adele, in August 1989. Sadly, I was still in a coma after my accident when Adele was born.

Chapter Four

Approaching the Accident

In 1989, just prior to my accident, I was working in the opencast mining business. I had been working for Balfour Beatty up at Glenfruin, Coulport, building the roads for the nuclear submarine base, when one of the companies working on the base – Banks – asked me to work on the opencast mine down near Broxburn. At the time, Coulport was a difficult place to access, and Balfour Beatty was building a road over the hills to improve the access. While working on their opencast project at Broxburn, Banks hit a seam of coal, but they couldn't extract it because they didn't have a license to do so. While they waited to obtain the license, their CAT 245 (excavator) was put out on hire to Balfour Beatty and I was asked if I wanted to drive it.

Ian Beattie, who was a general foreman for Banks, saw how I operated the 245 and asked me to work for them. He said that the next job with Balfour Beatty was at Castle Douglas and, as the weather was so bad down there, I'd be rained off more than I'd be working. In the opencast mining business work is never rained off because it's working with rock rather than soil. It was an easy decision for me and I was glad I made the move as Banks was a very good company.

It turned out that I was very happy at the opencast mine and Banks liked my work. I'd use the excavator to peel away the surface soil to expose the coal beneath, then I'd use a different machine to lift the coal. I quickly learnt how to do that and how to do it cleanly. I could take a whole seam out at a time without any need to wash it, which was beneficial to the company. If a digger driver takes out too much muck with the coal, then the coal has to be washed, which is an added expense, increases the time taken for the job and is bad for the environment. I really loved the opencast mine work, even though the job was tricky. I did a good job and Banks paid me top money.

Later that year, the telephone rang and my wife answered. It was two of the skydiving party who had gone to France with me. She handed me the receiver and I was asked if I could drive them to the drop zone at the old Errol airfield in Perthshire, a short distance away. Of course, I agreed. As I was driving, I noticed the wind picking up considerably and thought it would most likely buffer their jump. By the time I had dropped my friends at the drop zone, their excitement had infected me. I was about to head home when I heard a voice calling through the wind – it was Johnny, the chief instructor. "Donnie, I am not putting this aircraft up with only four people on board, but I'll put it up with five!" This was more than a hint and it put considerable pressure on me, especially with all the jumpers in earshot.

I apologetically replied, "Sorry to be a killjoy, but someone will come along soon to add to the flight number." That sort of thing happened quite often. I added, "I promised Marion that I'd be home for tea."

In an effort to tempt me, Johnny asked, "Donnie, would you like to jump with the Wildfire?" He continued, "In France you did everything right, first time. Besides, the wind right now is on the limits and will assist you in speed depreciation. Are you up for the challenge, or are you going to go home for your dinner and leave these guys standing there disappointed?"

That threw me into complete confusion. It was a dream offer and I felt a surge of adrenaline before I called back, "No, sorry! I've got to go." The moment I said those words, feelings of regret hit me.

The reply, designed to lay on the guilt, was, "Are you going to let us all down, then?"

"No ... but ..." I answered. I was torn between returning home to my family as I'd promised and fulfilling my skydiving ambition. I knew they were laughing and joking about me going home for my tea and being frightened to jump the wildfire. Finally, I gave in to temptation. If I was getting the chance of jumping the wildfire there was no way I would be giving u the chance, it looked so exciting 'WOW'. "Fire up that plane." I was committed to skydive with the Wildfire right there and then.

I pulled on my jumpsuit, put on the Wildfire and we all proceeded to the plane. My mind was racing and, in my head, I was repeating the mantra, 'New parachute, remember to leave 1,000 feet for the run-in. Always be aware of your altitude.' I was in safety and technical mode, as ever. Jumping height was set for 7,500 feet and as we reached it, I tentatively edged to the open door, with me and the Wildfire ready to jump into the blue yonder.

This was my chance and I was completely up for it – I was up for anything.

I edged closer and closer to the door and then I was away, free-falling. I was in my element – I turned, flipped and put into practice all my training brilliantly.

I felt as if the sky was made for me alone. Checking my altimeter once more, I opened the chute. Going from 120mph to full chute deployment in a split-second is a near-indescribable experience. The rush of speed under canopy is phenomenal. In this state of delight, I was shrieking all sorts of expletives, but no one other than me could hear them. As I was ecstatically plummeting through my descent, I recall repeating that essential doctrine to do a good run-in and to slow down; this was paramount.

The feeling I had was exactly why I had taken up the sport – it was thrilling. I glanced again at the windsock only to see it was empty of wind! Then the next second all was OK with a full windsock. 'What is happening? Full, empty, full? Don't panic, Donnie,' I assured myself. I have always prided myself on my fast thinking, but I knew the dearth of wind was a major hindrance to the safe completion of the jump, especially with the fast and fearsome Wildfire. Checking my altimeter again, I read 1,000 feet. I was now running-in, a term familiar to parachutists, and the ground was surging up to greet me. My meter indicated I was approaching 500 feet. A strong oncoming wind was essential, in fact, imperative, for this new canopy to function correctly and a glance at the windsock confirmed my worst fear. The wind was periodically gusting. Meanwhile I was hurtling downwards and I knew I was in serious trouble. My mind frantically scrabbled for a solution and I decided to flare the chute in an attempt to reduce my speed. It didn't work. I continued my descent at 100mph so that the only thing left for me to do was to prepare as best I could for the inevitable crash.

I landed and at first my feet skimmed the ground, leading to a brief moment when I thought, 'I'll be OK.'

It was a brief moment too because seconds later, as I closed my eyes and braced myself – *bang* – I hit the ground.

When this parachute first went on mainstream sale in 1989 (that fated year), it caused significant difficulties, even for skydivers who had more than 10,000 jumps under their belts. Incredibly, since then, that chute has been further developed to make it even smaller and therefore faster, with the aim of increasing the thrill of skydiving because the skydiver's appetite for that can never be satiated and techniques have been developed to slow/control these canopies.

Funnily enough, not long before the accident, I had persuaded my insurance company that skydiving was very safe, arguing that the most dangerous aspect of the sport was driving to the centre. Luckily, I had managed to secure my pension.

The first my family heard about my accident was when my sister received a phone call from Billy, saying, "Sheila, Donnie has had an accident and is in Dundee Royal Infirmary." Her immediate thought was that it was a car accident because she hadn't known I was jumping that day. Billy explained, in his calm, reassuring way, that it had been a skydiving accident. Sheila informed Marion, now seven months pregnant with Adele, and they gathered together some of my things to take to the hospital. My mother, who was visiting us, chose to stay to look after Mark, who was just a baby. They assumed it was nothing worse than a bruised ego and a few bumps, cuts and grazes.

Completely unaware of how serious it was, Sheila and Marion drove to the hospital at a leisurely pace, chatting away, singing along to the songs on the radio. Amidst the frivolity, while amusing themselves at the thought of my injured pride, Marion thought she heard something on the radio and it was to do with skydiving. The bulletin became their focus, as they listened intently with the volume raised. The news reported how a man had fallen 7,500 feet, was critically injured and was being airlifted to hospital. They heard that the airlift was heading for the same hospital as the one to which they were travelling.

They felt sorry for this skydiver – after all, they knew the skydiving gang through watching me jump on so many occasions, and their first reaction was that they couldn't wait to tell me what had happened. Then, as each detail was disclosed, a sense of deep dread began to spread over them. Sheila brought the car to a halt as they exclaimed in unison, "Donnie!"

Chapter Five

Recovery

On the neurological ward, a nurse was asked the question, "Excuse me, can I bother you a moment?"

"Oh my God," she shouted excitedly. "I don't believe this!"

She ran to gather all her colleagues – the neurosurgeons and consultants too – and they gathered around the patient's bed before phoning the family, who immediately sped 22 miles to be at the bedside. That patient was me and those words I said to the nurse that day were the first I had uttered since the accident in mid-summer. It was now autumn.

By all accounts, no one had expected me to survive long. My condition was so severe, with multiple spinal injuries, that it was miraculous I was even breathing, let alone talking. Everyone was so excited and, at that point, those closest to me knew I was on my way back. From late June of that year until late October my capability to communicate had been entirely impossible and I cannot really remember waking up after my accident. What I do know of those months is from what others have told me. They said my family were always at my side, praying and hoping that I could find the strength to bring myself out of the coma, to give some sort of sign – a flutter of the eyelid, or even the tiniest of twitches – to show their prayers were being answered.

The air ambulance had taken me to Dundee Royal Infirmary, where I remained in a coma. Despite what the neurosurgeon was telling her, Marion seemed to know I was OK and could tell my brain was still working. My problem was that I could hear people, but I couldn't respond. Even so, I knew I would get there because I had that faith. It was torture, though, listening to the doctors and not being able to respond. I remember lying in the hospital bed thinking, 'I know Marion believes I will speak again.' That gave me hope and was probably what led to me talking to that nurse.

Due to my great resilience and rapid rate of progression, it was decided by the neurosurgeons that I was ready to be transferred to a hospital more local to home that provided a suitable rehabilitation unit. I can remember being transferred by ambulance from Dundee Royal Infirmary to Ward 5 of the Bridge of Earn Hospital, which I suppose is my first clear memory from that time, yet it was a year after the accident. Everything prior to that is a blank in my mind. Of course, I still couldn't talk or walk, but I remember there was a young boy on the ward who had lost both of his legs and I thought to myself how lucky I was to still have mine. Despite the other issues I was facing, at least my body was intact.

The new hospital pleased my family for a couple of reasons. First, they knew I was not stuck bed-bound in a care home and, second, it was only about five miles away from my family, which made it much easier for them to visit me. The time I had spent in Dundee Royal Infirmary had been very tough on my family because they'd had to travel to Dundee to see me, sometimes several times a day. I know it took a lot out of them. The family was in Perth, but Marion couldn't drive at the time, so she had to be driven by them to the hospital. My family fought for me not to be transferred to a care home, despite the neurological consensus that I should be, but, thankfully, one senior neurosurgeon refused to agree to it. At that point, the decision was taken to take me to Bridge of Earn Hospital. As for me, I couldn't wait to embrace this new challenge and I resolved to have victory over the damage that had been caused.

I remember lying in the hospital bed, hearing the doctors describing my condition. I would shake my head, convinced that what they were saying was not true. Everyone was telling me that I had to accept it, but I couldn't. For every one neurosurgeon who looked at me and said I would be all right, another 10 disagreed, saying I would never recover and would be a "vegetable" for the rest of my life and even if I did manage to get out of the hospital, a top eye doctor said my eye injuries were incurable and, in his opinion, I'd never drive again. Marion knew how determined I was, though, and she asked people not to speak like that in front of me.

The pain I was in was the simple but constant reminder to me that I had to heal. I strove to transform that pain into action, partly because I had no alternative, but it was a huge challenge. Nevertheless, it was one I was determined to rise to. The hospital environment was comfortable and I was as happy as I could be in that situation, feeling cared for, as though I was back in my childhood home. At times, though, my incapacity made me angry; all I wanted was to be able to look out of a window like anyone else. If ever I felt too downhearted and without hope, I would tell myself, 'Get a grip, Donnie!' I knew I had to continue the battle. Even being able to nod when offered a cup of tea was a huge achievement, but the effort would so exhaust me that I would then fall asleep.

Ever since I was first in the hospital, Marion had ensured I had plenty of visitors at my bedside. Never a day passed without some family presence and Marion was devoted in her attentions. I recall the nurses commenting about the steady stream of visitors, although I wasn't fully conscious of all that was going. Work colleagues loyally came along too, demanding that I return back to work immediately to maintain company production levels and standards. At that, everyone chuckled, as did I, but I soon paid the price in the form of a sharp pain. Thank God for those injections and the drugs.

I was quite hard on myself because I felt so useless, just lying there – a burden if ever there was one. I was restless, impatient and desperate to achieve more movement. Sheila, Rita (my mother) and Marion were acutely aware of how hard I was working to achieve this, monitoring every attempt I made to improve my movement, however slight. I saw the tears in their eyes as they watched me struggle and that made me even more determined to succeed because I had to do it for them.

They would try to sooth me too, telling me to relax or to be more patient. I knew that they were being influenced by the professional opinion that it was highly unlikely I would ever be anything other than bedridden and I couldn't blame them. I knew I had to hold onto all my positivity if I was going to come out of it all successfully. Then I remembered something and it became a pillar of strength for me. The senior neurosurgeon had said, some weeks prior, "Don't write this man off; he has a lot of fight in him!"

My positive attitude was re-emerging from deep within me.

In due course, an occupational therapist was assigned to me to re-establish basic physiological processes. Considering what a tiresome patient I must have been, she had an unfailing enthusiasm and I was determined to shine for her. She'd hold and direct my hand, clasping my fingers as we would together undo the top button of my pyjama tunic. Soon enough, all were undone. It was such a simple task but it demonstrated that I was making terrific progress. It went so well, we even managed to put a new set of pyjamas on me that day. This became a daily routine for a few hours at a time. For me, it was like a full day's work – very painful and very tiring. After several days of steady improvement, I was proficient in brushing my teeth without there being too much mess everywhere and I could also eat soup and drink tea. Success! It wasn't too long until I could do it without needing the protection of a bib.

Then there was the speech therapist who visited two or three times a week. The serious head and spinal injuries I'd suffered had resulted in an inability to speak coherently, with the most I could manage being slurred groans and growls. I'd be instructed to identify, for example, a dog, cat or a tiger from picture cards held in front of me, but all that came out were meaningless mumbles accompanied by little water spouts of saliva. Bizarrely, the first words to be articulated properly were expletives. Swearing became a reward in itself, the words creating the stepping stones towards the simple communication of "yes", "no", "thanks" and "please", etc.

After a few weeks, I was ready for the physiotherapist and when it was time for my first session, I was bundled into a wheelchair by two nurses. There were to be three sessions each week and I was eager to embark on this new stage of my recovery. Even though I had been given some strong drugs, I was aware there was a risk I might have a fit but those nurses were both very careful and very attentive. On one day when I was taken for a session, I remember one of the nurses saying, "I don't know how your wife would manage." I thought that my wife would probably manage fine, but her comment did serve as a subtle indication to me just how seriously injured I was. Things simply were not the same and I had to adjust to this reality.

The therapist was a guy, very good at his job and with masses of experience. In fact, I still bump into him now and then and he always reminds me of those difficult days and my remarkable recovery. His task was to encourage basic movement in me so that I could regain some independence. My right arm was locked at a right angle, while my right leg was as straight as a board and wouldn't bend at all. After studying the brain scan, the specialists said this was down to severe muscular spasms that were distorting the messages to the brain, thereby preventing physiological co-ordination. In contrast, my left arm and leg both had much more movement. The team placed some very light weights on my palms and then they manipulated me, only stopping when my extreme grimace indicated I was in agony. This was to be routine practice and there was no avoiding it. Essentially, I had to overcome the pain barrier. Each session was exhausting, to the point that I'd often nod off between attempts, and on return to my bed on the ward, I'd immediately fall fast asleep.

After a few weeks, my physio programme was upped to five half-days per week, interspersed with writing exercises from the occupational therapist and more speech therapy. I was certainly a busy boy but, all the while, I was gradually improving in these areas. I've always been right-handed, but I was instructed to change to using my left hand, much to my annoyance. I suppose I was being stubborn or maybe I didn't want to give in, but I point blank refused to learn to write with my left hand. I was angry and felt the physios were bullies for forcing this on me. I was adamant I'd be writing with my right hand again and, when I did, it would be better than ever. In an effort to rebel, using my right hand with my arm still locked at the elbow, I scrawled with a pencil on some paper. It was a valiant effort but futile – my triangles had no angles and my circles were little more than squiggles.

In another little act of rebellion, I insisted that my morning coffee be served in a proper mug, not a plastic beaker. Even though it was heavier, I took great delight in using its handle to lift it up to my mouth and then lower it again, without spilling a single drop (well, mostly, but that's true of everyone). Each time I did it, I gained more confidence and it was an achievement that gave me pleasure, almost like a little game I'd play each morning. The best thing was that I'd always win because my strength and dexterity were slowly being restored.

Morning and night, I'd train myself. In bed, when the lights were out, I began implementing a little routine I had created, during which I'd regularly perform a sequence of lifting my legs and arms as high as I could, using the sheets as counterweights. I had to be very discreet when doing this because I wasn't permitted to do anything on my own, having been caught initially and told off for doing so. I didn't stop, though, because I knew it was all going to contribute to my recovery.

I wanted to walk as soon as it was feasible. On one visit to the physio unit, the team brought me to my feet, out of the wheelchair, and had me standing, with support, to strengthen my leg muscles. They didn't know how strong these muscles were or how practised I was, thanks to my little twice-daily in-bed exercises. In fact, I felt so strong that I started to stamp on the spot only to be reprimanded because it was considered beyond my stage of capability. Once again, I'd protest at this perceived negativity by shaking my head in defiance as an addition to my new stamping routine. What did they know? As far as I was concerned, I was in training for marathons and skydiving again.

Unfortunately, my elation at my new-found strength was soon punctured when I was informed that my left eye was so badly damaged it required an operation as a matter of urgency. I had thought that all my problems were on the right side of my body and my mood didn't improve when I was told I would need three corrective operations on my eye and there was a high risk I could lose it entirely. As it turned out, the ophthalmologist at Bridge of Earn, an eye surgeon, managed the operation in one attempt, during which he removed the eye from its socket, operated on the eye muscle and then put the eye back in again. Fortunately for me, he was one of the very best in the country – another thing to be thankful for. However, after the surgery, I was left with only partial vision, a large blind spot and tunnel vision. The eye surgeon said that was the way it was going to be for the rest of my life, assuring me that he had done everything possible. He said I would always be partially blind.

"Sorry," he said. "You've got that for life."

Marion, behind the scenes, was frequently nagging the medical staff to allow me to return home, even if only for a few hours. As I improved, Marion pushed for me to go home at the weekends because all my treatments were during the week, which meant I was left in the hospital doing nothing on Saturdays and Sundays. She convinced the nurses and the doctors that she could take care of me. They understood and let me out on Friday evenings, on the condition that I would go back in on the Monday. She had an extra reason for doing this because while I was in my coma, she had given birth for the second time producing a little girl and a sister for Mark. When I had come out of the coma, Marion and Mark had come to my bedside, Marion with a little bundle in her arms. At first glance, I could see my grandmother Kaleena in my baby daughter Adele. I knew that was her name and all the while when I had been drifting in and out of the coma, my family and friends had been playing cassette tapes of my little gurgling Adele. Those sounds must have had some effect on me because later, when I was alone in bed, I'd recall the audio and feel that I knew my baby daughter.

No doubt, at times, Marion must have regretted having me at home because she already had her hands full with young Mark and Adele, so the last thing she needed was another baby, albeit one aged 27, around the house. I had continuous visitors, too, when good friends and work colleagues came to the house to remember old stories and tell jokes. They'd have me in stitches. They do say laughter is the best medicine and those visitors were as valuable as doctors and nurses to me. I feel so grateful to have an adoring family and so fortunate to have true friends.

After I had been in Bridge of Earn for about nine months, I was allowed to move home full time, having to return to the hospital every morning for the various treatments, which continued as before. Luckily, I was making significant progress, so I was quite relaxed about it all.

One day, as I was waiting for treatment, John, one of my old friends, came walking into the hospital.

"What are you doing here?" I asked, surprised to see him at the hospital.

"Donnie?" John replied. "What are *you* doing here?"

It turned out that John too had had an accident and was receiving physiotherapy for his injuries. We were good friends from years back and as John lived near my home, we started travelling together to the hospital for daily treatments. Having some company on the journey – someone I could talk to and laugh with – really helped.

My progress was good, but I was often irked by the consistent chastisement from the physio staff. I wanted to develop my muscles and longed for more weights, so I'd exercise with an empty barbell, for example, but then request that they made it tougher. They, however, insisted weights were not appropriate because my arm was locked as a result of severe muscular spasm and had to be treated in a certain way due to the brain damage.

There was, however, a significant and practical impasse between my brain damage and what I wanted to do. Dad could see the agony I was in because my back was in such a sorry state that it was torment every time I tried to move. I was struggling to walk, constantly falling all over the place, which only made things worse. Dad had previously suffered from problems with his back and had obtained some relief from an excellent osteopath who lived near him by the name of Raymond Robson. I had been at school with Raymond's sons. They had a garage down in Auchterarder and I used to take my car to them for repairs when Dad was too busy to do them. As far as Dad was concerned, no expense would be spared to bring on my recovery and my poor father dug far deeper than he should have or could have been expected to do. He thought Raymond was the best and he wanted me to benefit from his treatment.

In our first session, Raymond sat me down on a stool and then started pressing, prodding and pushing up and down my spine. He said it would be sore, but I was still strongly medicated so didn't feel much. At the end, he said he was pleased with what he'd done and that after the initial discomfort had subsided, I would feel great. He was true to his word because I felt better than I had in a long time, I was no longer so hunched up and seemed much freer in my body generally.

He turned his attention to my locked arm and asked what the hospital had said about it. I told him the diagnosis but as he felt my arm, he said, "There is something else up here. Brace yourself, Donnie, because this might be sore." He then told me to stretch out my arm. I was convinced that would be impossible, but as he pulled on it, my arm slowly straightened. I was astonished. Then he transferred to my straight right leg, which was locked rigid. He tweaked, pulled, jerked and twisted it at the knee, explaining that this procedure was very tricky, made harder by my physical stature. Then he suddenly grabbed my knee and gave it a wrench. There was an audible click as my leg folded at a right angle and my foot dropped to the floor as though I was sitting normally on a chair. He had unlocked my leg, leaving me stunned, relieved and very happy. It transpired that both my locked arm and leg were essentially non-muscular issues and had been wholly bone-related, which was why osteopathy had been deemed the best therapy to try. I was also receiving homeopathic treatment from Carol at the same time and the combined effect was fantastic.

The ambulance soon arrived at home to return me to the rehabilitation unit for continued therapy as part of my recovery plan. It was early in the morning and I walked to the front door with Marion. The ambulance pulled up and the ramp was put down. It was the usual driver and, of course, he was expecting to have to push me on board in the wheelchair. You can imagine his expression when he saw me, with a grin from ear to ear, approaching the vehicle, on my own, upright and pushing my wheelchair ahead of me. He looked as though he'd seen a mirage.

Monday mornings were allocated for swimming and I duly performed, with fancy little flips, twists and turns that I couldn't do before. I was, however, warned that the hospital staff wouldn't be happy that I'd gone to an osteopath, whereas I had thought they'd be as pleased as me. After swimming, I had my usual cup of tea at 10am and discovered I was the talk of the place. A nurse soon approached, saying I was to go to the office of the head doctor of the rehabilitation unit.

I began heading for the office, pushing the wheelchair in front of me. I felt so good, I could have picked it up and swung it around as a dance partner.

I could have danced all night, I was that elated. A secretary greeted me and I was ushered into a room. The head doctor got up from his desk and, having greeted me, sat me down on a chair opposite his and closed the door. The first thing he said was, "Donnie, what are you doing? The whole hospital is talking about you."

I replied, "Am I doing anything wrong?" News of my osteopathic treatment had spread like, well, wildfire.

He said, "I'm not saying you have done anything wrong, but, you know, Donnie, natural therapists embarrass us! They can do things we simply have not been trained to do!"

I returned to the tearoom, still pushing my chair. My good mood was evident and it subsequently had a positive effect on the development of my speech but, of course, even more so in physiotherapy sessions. It was all so much easier and I wanted to do more but was again reminded to exercise patience. The staff were, nevertheless, stunned with the new improved Donnie compared with the incapacitated Donnie of the previous week. My tasks were tailored to my new state, with the result I found them more meaningful and satisfying.

It is a notable characteristic within my family that we always try to do our best no matter what it might be. Sheila, my brother Gary and I were always up at the crack of dawn as children, while Mum and Dad would be off to work. One designated chore was to light the coal fire using kindling. (Although Sheila liked to stay in bed a little longer, only getting up after I had lit it and then claiming she'd got up to do it herself.) Perhaps this routine helped instil an element of discipline and motivation that was further entrenched by the routine of walking three miles to school in the morning, in all weathers, and the same again at the end of the day. I'd have to toddle off on my own because it would have done nothing for Sheila's street cred for her to be seen with her pesky little brother. However, due to Sheila's renowned allure, there were many who'd offer her lifts everywhere and that was a much-appreciated benefit for me. We bonded very well, while it was different for Gary because he was much younger.

We were a family of the countryside, living in beautiful Perthshire with all its rivers and glens. I'd go fishing regularly with my uncle and he taught me karate. I, in turn, taught Gary – I maintain I did it very gently, but he disagrees. In hot weather, we used to swim in the lochs and rivers, paying some heed to the warnings of danger from the adults watching over us, as they sat on chairs with cups of tea, having their picnic. My schoolteacher made it her mission, because of where we lived, to teach us to swim to a level of some proficiency. She had us competing against each other for certificates. I have always striven to do better than the others.

Chapter Six

Rehabilitation

After the operation, my eye was healing well and the surgeon had produced good results, leaving me with coordinated eye movement, to my great joy. I was feeling sufficiently encouraged by the results to address the remaining blind spot in my vision, even though the eye surgeon had categorically asserted, however, that it was something I'd have to live with. I wasn't going to give up that easily.

I'd had a further series of treatments with Raymond the osteopath as well, again delivering remarkable movement that meant I could walk unsupported, although I still had to use walking aids, which I detested. I continued to have twitches, twinges and pain in my back but, as my osteopath kept reminding me, I had fallen 7,500 feet, so it was to be expected.

I was now spending nights at home with Marion and days back at hospital rehabilitation. I was also receiving osteopathy, of course, and I happened to call one day for an appointment regarding the pain in my back. Unfortunately, it transpired that Raymond was in hospital himself, so I scanned the telephone directory for another osteopath and then it struck me. I spotted an advert for natural therapy. Words I'd heard before – "natural therapists embarrass us" – immediately came to mind, so I called the number to arrange an appointment for the following morning.

The advert was for a man named John Page, who was a cranial osteopath. He had a very good reputation and was one of the best in Europe. The difference that man made to my life is immense. Today, when I hear people talking about their situation and saying there is nothing to be done for their condition, I always think there *is* something they can do and that is to see John Page. I was so lucky to find him and, even today, it is amazing to think what he achieved with my condition. If it were not for him, I would be nothing. The story of how he helped me regain my eyesight is a typical one when talking about John Page.

He explained to me how the human body works, how there are more than 360 bones in the head etc. He said that bones in the wrong position prevent everything from flowing. Being a cranial osteopath, he was more interested in my head injuries than anything else and, at that stage, my speech was still poor and very slurred. He started by massaging my skull, subtly moving the bones and, initially, I was disappointed because, unlike with Raymond, I hadn't noticed any immediate benefit from the session. Nevertheless, he reassured me. "I'm only starting on the process," he said. "There is plenty to do over the next few weeks and you will see it get better over time."

Throughout the series of appointments, every so often major breakthroughs were achieved. On one occasion, he asked how my speech was developing and as I began to answer, I suddenly realised my reply was tripping off my tongue. I was speaking almost normally again and a wide smile spread across my face. Soon all the stiffness in my body had dissipated – it was amazing – and I was mentally sharper, too.

I recall I was snapping my fingers, in a small eureka way, because an idea had come to me. I knew I had to ask him about my vision issues.

"John," I said, "is there anything you can do for the blind spot in my eyes?"

"This is incredible," he said. "I only heard this week about a treatment for that being carried out in America."

That was typical of John Page. He always learning about new treatments and had such a positive approach to his patients. To my surprise, he put on a pair of surgical gloves and proceeded to fumble about in my mouth for about a quarter of an hour. He then removed the gloves and felt my head, before putting them on again and delving once more inside my mouth. He repeated this procedure a few times, feeling the roof of my mouth, until he finally announced, "I've done some major work there, Donnie. Just wait and see what happens over the next week."

Later that night, Marion and I were preparing to go over to Sheila's house for dinner. Marion was getting ready, while I was watching the television and she was trying to make me hurry. I turned to tell her I was on my way and suddenly noticed I could see the light from the television, which was on my right side. Until that point, I had been blind on that side, but now there was light. Was I beginning to regain my full field of vision?

I had read somewhere how important it is to work the area where you have poor vision, to exercise to help restore your sight, so I kept looking at the telly through my right-hand side field of vision, trying to drag my eyes back to working again. John Page had also said that the brain needs to relearn how to see, so I would turn my head to the left to watch the television from the right. It was my way of teaching the brain to repair my vision. John did some more work on my head and soon I was seeing light and colours again in that previously blocked field of vision. It was an incredible feeling. I'd had all the experts telling me I was never going to regain my sight, but suddenly I was beginning to see again.

In a matter of weeks, I went down for my driver's eligibility examination at the Astley Ainslie Hospital, Edinburgh. During the medical examination, the doctors used the same machine that the eye surgeon had used a year earlier. This time, however, they were obtaining completely different results. The assessment examiners were astonished because there was no blind spot. The doctor was dumbfounded that John Page could have made such a difference, but the evidence was clearly there in front of him. My driving license was sanctioned and it duly came through the post.

My determination and positive attitude, combined with John Page's treatment, had returned my sight to normal. I once again had the freedom to get around using my car. Added to that, I wasn't in a wheelchair any longer, though I was still using the sticks. I was determined to avoid making myself look and feel any more disabled than was necessary, so I only used the sticks when I really had to. However, I made the most of being able to drive. In my view, it's essential to maintain a positive outlook on life and concentrate on the things you *can* do, not those you can't. I'd visit good friends in the area and they'd be so glad to see me, happy that I had emerged from the abyss against all the odds.

Darcey, an old friend from the trip to France, was especially pleased to see me. He called me one day from Edinburgh, asking me for a lift. He was going skydiving, at the place of my accident. I'd been there several times since it had happened and I had no qualms about going there. I still loved skydiving because it was me using the Wildfire parachute that was dangerous and not the sport itself. However, I was strangely uncomfortable when talking to the other jumpers. I felt inferior, stupid, as if it had been due to my own ineptitude that I'd had the accident.

When I was taking Darcey back home he was staying at another Skydiving mates - Kenny, who owned The Gothy in Kelty. A good pub. A busy local. Darcy said to me "you should have been told the truth about your accident", we sat in the pub and he said "Donnie I feel terrible the accident was not your fault you should be suing the club". He told me about that fateful day. I found all that he told me very interesting. He said that he felt a lot better after his discussions with me and that it would upset a few people but tough.

That day was not a good one because when I returned home, I learnt that I was to lose my license for good. The eye surgeon had advised the driving authorities that, due to the final diagnosis of a blind spot that could not be improved by medical treatment, my license should be rescinded. The driving board admitted over the phone that their documentation showed the amazing improvements that cranial osteopathy had achieved but they told me they were obliged to ban me from driving for ever because the eye surgeon's word was final and they had no authority to overrule it.

However, through this gloom, there was a glimmer of light. I was told there was one person in the country with the authority to overrule it and I had six months within which to contact this person if I wasn't to lose my license at all. I asked my GP to arrange an appointment, which he did, but the bad news was that, due to this man's workload, it wouldn't be for two years. Between that time and the appointment date, I did indeed lose my driving license. Marion, the kids and I were all devastated as we knew I had no vision issues. In conjunction with my lawyer, we managed, eventually, to revoke that decision and I regained my driving license. I only got my license back after being declared fit to drive by the top eye doctor – the man I had waited for two years to have an appointment with.

After leaving Bridge of Earn Hospital, I was living full time in Perth with my family, while also going to see John Page for therapy sessions. There was a massive difference between the crippled wreck I had been – a man who couldn't walk or talk, who was blind and disabled – and the person who could take care of himself once more. It is hard to believe it all, even today. It may sound funny, but I could literally see the changes John and Carol were making to my life. John was making a massive difference with the cranial osteopathy and the homoeopathic treatment from Carol was fine-tuning what he'd done, putting the finishing touches to his work if you like. John could be carrying out a treatment on my skull, but I'd feel the sensation in my feet. That was how it was with John; my whole body would react powerfully to his treatments and Carol was getting the information from my feet. John and Carol (she is a cranial osteopath as well as a homeopath) sometimes worked on me together and that was amazing beyond belief. The treatments took a huge amount out of me, but I used to be out cold while they worked on me, drifting off to sleep while they worked.

Both Carol and John work at the Upledger Institute in Florida and I'm now determined to go there for some intensive treatment. I can only imagine what it must be like having six therapists working on you at the same time. Whenever people ask about my recovery, I put in a good word for the Upledger Institute. The treatments and positive attitude obtained from these types of therapies are vital in any strong programme of rehabilitation. That therapy has put me where I am today, and I can say that without a word of a lie.

I felt I was nearing the finishing line of my recovery, although I was continuing, whenever it could be afforded, my treatment with the cranial osteopath. Physically, I was almost there but I knew my mental stated required some further help. During that time, I read in the newspaper about Paul McKenna, the hypnotist, and, somehow, I knew that I had to see him.

Before my accident, my life had been full of fun; I had enjoyed working and playing hard, I had loved skydiving, going to the football and having fun with my mates. As far as I was concerned, there was nothing I couldn't have done in those days. I was a young man with all my life ahead of me and I was determined to enjoy it. During my recovery, I wanted that high level of positivity back in my life and in Paul McKenna I recognised someone who could help me. I called his office in Leicester and, as if by magic, my call was answered by none other than the man himself. He arranged for me to go to London to participate in one of his seminars, which I did.

I found myself sitting in an audience of about 200 people, while McKenna started to tell us all about a man who'd made a miraculous recovery from a near-fatal skydiving accident. Unbeknown to me, his team had done some detailed background research on me and, moreover, my positive attitude throughout my rehabilitation was seen as testimony to achieving the impossible. He spoke of the difference between the man who had first spoken to him and the man now sitting in the audience. "The only reason Donnie is the way he is today is because of his attitude," Paul said, and he was right. It is all about self-belief and having a positive attitude.

He pulled me aside afterwards and said, "Donnie, I think you should meet Dr Richard Bandler." Dr Bandler is an American doctor and expert in self-help techniques. He is also the man who created neuro-linguistic programming (NLP), a method, to put it as simply as possible, of reprogramming your brain to do things you had not thought possible before the treatment. It is also used by Paul McKenna in his sessions. As the practitioner talks, you listen, and the way they talk reprogrammes your brain. This takes place over a four-day seminar – you sit and listen while the practitioner works on your way of thinking.

An incredible feat of the NLP sessions is that there can be another 200 or so people in the room, each of them learning, just as you are, to think and do things differently. Dr Bandler was soon to visit Edinburgh and I managed to secure a place at a series of sessions. After one morning session with Dr Bandler, I remember I sat down at lunchtime with a lady who was in a similar situation to me. "I can't believe it," she said. "Here am I, after years of seeing psychiatrists without any improvements and, after one morning with this man, I am a different person."

She explained that she had paid a psychiatrist for 14 sessions of treatment without any success, but after the one morning with Dr Bandler, she felt better than she had ever done before. I saw Dr Bandler for three days in all. He does everything by seminar and he works on everyone in the room simultaneously without them even knowing he is doing the therapy. Paul McKenna said to me that Dr Bandler was on a different level and he was right. NLP tied in perfectly with all the other treatments I was having, and I cannot speak highly enough of the difference it made. In a way, it brought everything together and gave me the strength to be who I am.

Together Dr Bandler and Paul McKenna seemed to have transmitted some sort of pulse into my inner psychological make-up that had connected with my positive attitude. The outcome of my time with both men is absolutely incredible when you think about it. They got me back on track to a positive way of thinking and improved my attitude to life, allowing me to gain strength and confidence by focusing on the right parts of my life.

The real secret of NLP for me is that you do not even know it is happening because it is simply working away in the background, helping you every day. All this was going on while I was still a patient at Bridge of Earn Hospital and the changes in my condition were immense over those months, to the extent that when I was with my occupational therapist and the doctors in the hospital, they could not believe what they were seeing.

Chapter Seven

Becoming Myself Again

For anyone reading this, it is essential to realise how bad my life was after my accident. My future was bleak and I was in a dark place. Looking back today, I cannot recognise that man compared with the one I have become and it is all down to the positive attitude I took on and the treatments from Paul McKenna, John Page and Dr Richard Bandler. The way I see it is that all the people who helped me are tied together; they are part of the package that transformed me back into the man I was before my accident. I am, of course, physically disabled, but I know there is nothing I cannot overcome, nothing that can hold me back and it is all thanks to my positive attitude to life.

Of the five people who started skydiving that first day in June 1985, Grant and I were the only ones who continued with the sport. Grant was still skydiving up until a couple of years ago and he must have thousands of jumps under his belt. We keep in touch even now because you build up a real bond with people when you are skydiving together regularly. It's probably because we love the adrenaline rush and can see it in other people; we are addicted to it, I suppose.

Much has been written about my accident, with articles in the national and local newspapers featuring me and my story. Journalists wrote about my fall and how I had survived against the odds. Marion was very good at cutting out the articles and keeping them safe for people to read, but then, one day, I lost my rag and threw them in the bin. It was depressing, seeing all the stories about me never walking again. I knew I did not need that negativity around the house and I was right to do it at the time. Today, though, I think it would be good to have them as a reference point, as something that shows the place I was in then so that it can be compared with where I am today.

When I had my accident and started to show signs of recovery, back in the late 1980s and early 1990s, all the therapies that helped me were still in their infancy. These days, people are very aware of positive thinking. They know about Paul McKenna's hypnotherapy and even the cranial osteopathy from John Page. Back when I was in recovery, though, those therapies were not so common and I was very lucky to have had access to them.

A year after the accident, I drove to Dundee Royal Infirmary – this was six months after I had been written off as a "vegetable". The staff went crazy and couldn't get over the rate of my recovery. A similar moment happened at the Kirkstyle Inn, a pub in Mum's village of Dunning, which held a fundraising meal for the air ambulance. They do this every year and other towns do the same.

We went along – Mum, Marion and other friends and family – as the air ambulance crew were the people who had saved my life. The personnel who had rescued me on the day of my accident were there and they could not believe that I was the same person they had taken to the Dundee Royal Infirmary only a year earlier. I'm not sure what they were expecting, but I doubt it was me in the great shape I was in by that night. They had seen me at my worst and had probably feared for the worst too, especially with their experience of dealing with severely injured people.

Chapter Eight

Final Thoughts

As my memory returned, I found I still had some confusion in my head over what happened. In my mind, there was no way I could have had my accident when skydiving, no way at all as far as I was concerned, and it is the same with other people who jump all the time. Skydiving is safe; I loved doing the jumps and I had done more than 60 error-free dives. Skydiving takes your level of excitement up another notch. It really is incredible. It is extremely safe and the statistics prove it. When an accident does happen, it is nearly always down to the skydiver not doing something correctly. As with anything in life, if you don't do everything as you should, something can go wrong.

Experienced divers, such as Grant, who was on the plane with me on my first jumps, have thousands of dives under their belts and have never had an accident. I became convinced that the accident couldn't have happened when skydiving. It was only after reading all the newspaper articles Marion had cut out and kept that I started to see that it was, indeed, a skydiving accident that had got me.

The point of this book is not only to tell people about my recovery and for them be inspired by my story, but also for them to know that there is help out there if it is needed. The most significant part of a good recovery, as Paul McKenna says, is *you*.

The patient's positive attitude and their willingness to fight for recovery are everything. Marion knew I was frustrated and she used to say, "Just accept it, Donnie." It was her way of trying to help me find where I was in life at that time. I used to answer, "Marion, I've never just accepted where I am in life. Even before the accident, I was always pushing myself, so why should it be any different now?" Paul McKenna says that my attitude was what got me through it all and it is what keeps me going today.

After my accident, I tried going back to working in the plant industry. Many people were telling me to take it easy, insisting that I was pushing myself too much, but that is my way. I was falling over frequently and drinking Red Bull in an effort to keep awake, which is not a good idea. It is all well and good to push yourself, but you have to give yourself a break from time to time too. My problem, I suppose, was that I didn't appreciate I didn't have the same capabilities after my accident that I'd had before it.

I'm pleased to say that my family are doing well. Adele helps run a business, working three days a week, and she is also busy raising her daughter. She qualified with an honour's degree in law, but she didn't want to do the apprenticeship to become a solicitor. Marion and I have never had to worry about Adele because she never suffers fools gladly. She is very like my sister Sheila in that way, although my mates say, "No, Donnie, she is just like you." Adele is always in charge and that was how it was when she was growing up.

Our son Mark is the spit of me, but more like his mother in personality. He works as a joiner and concentrates on taking care of his kids. I'm lucky enough to have three grandchildren. Mark and his partner Joanne have two children, Bonnie and Harris, and Adele and Conor have a daughter, Ivy Rose. Mark lives in Thornhill, and Adele is in Stirling, so I get to see my grandkids quite often.

To this day, I continue to strive, in my own way, determined to fully recover from the accident. Often, though, I feel embarrassed by what my injuries cause me to do, but there has been so much progress towards complete independence and I can now make my own coffee with no assistance (even if I serve it to myself on the counter at times). Ha! Ha! Take note, Donnie. I never focus on what is wrong and I also know that any setbacks I encounter will not obstruct me in my march to full recovery. This in no small part is due to my determination to defy the odds, along with the fantastic assistance of the NHS and my very special support team.

Every morning, as part of my routine, I visit the local coffee shop where I meet with a group of friends who have become a pillar of strength to me. We call ourselves the Coffee Crew. I could not wish for a greater help. After that, despite the caffeine and the laughs, I feel overwhelmingly tired and have to go home for a nap to prevent myself from dropping off right there in the café. I'm usually awakened but what is an alarm if not a signal to get up? I will not be contained within the damned comfort zone that tries to confine me.

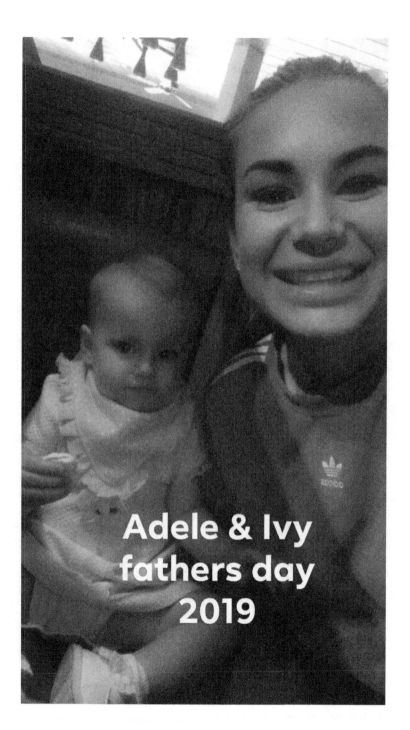

Adele & Ivy
fathers day
2019

Bonnie, Harris,& Ivy

Harris

Freefall –
Pushing it to the Edge

Donnie MacDougall

Printed in Great Britain
by Amazon

20854595R00048